GW01238126

Blockchain

The Ultimate Guide To The World Of Blockchain Technology

Ikuya Takashima

ISBN: 1978417918
ISBN-13: 9781978417915

TABLE OF CONTENTS

Introduction

Thank you for taking the time to purchase this book: The Ultimate Guide to the world of Blockchain Technology. This book covers the exciting topic of blockchain technology. It will teach you what blockchain technology is, how it works and how it could change your life completely.

Now, you probably have heard something about Bitcoin. Do you know exactly what it is though? Bitcoin is interesting, and we will give you some information about it here.

What is more interesting is the underlying infrastructure that makes Bitcoin work. The blockchain is so much more than just what makes Bitcoin work, though, it is an entirely new way of storing and securing data.

Blockchain makes it possible to keep your data out of the hands of hackers in a way that you would never have dreamed of. We're going to go through that so that you understand precisely how it does this.

We will then also discuss the advantages and disadvantages of the blockchain, and what the future looks like for it.

We are also going to go through what Ethereum is and how it relates to the blockchain. We will look at how Ethereum makes your life easier with smart contracts and how it is fostering creativity by facilitating the development of Dapps.

Let's get to it and learn more about this fascinating subject.

Chapter 1: What Is The Blockchain?

In this chapter, we'll start off slowly. We will go through what the blockchain is, what makes it secure and how it differs from traditional security methods.

There is a lot of information flying around the internet now about the blockchain and bitcoin and how blockchain will revolutionize our lives. But, before we get into all of that, let's look at what blockchain is.

To quote Investopedia[1], "A blockchain is a digitized, decentralized, public ledger of all cryptocurrency transactions. Constantly growing as 'completed' blocks (the most recent transactions) are recorded and added to it in chronological order, it allows market participants to keep track of digital currency transactions without central recordkeeping. Each node (a computer connected to the

---

[1] http://www.investopedia.com/terms/b/blockchain.asp

network) gets a copy of the blockchain, which is downloaded automatically."

But let's make it even simpler. A blockchain is, at its most basic, a computer structure or a place to keep data. A blockchain consists of data that is assembled into blocks, or units.

Each block is like the page of a book. Each "page" follows in sequence, and you can quickly see if a page has been removed by looking through the page numbers. The information on each "page" is ordered in a logical, chronological manner.

The pages are all bound together and form part of the same book. And, as with any library, there can be many other books as well.

With the blockchain, each new block is linked to the previous one in a logical sequence. You cannot delete a single transaction unless you can rewrite the whole chain after it as well.

That may not seem like a big deal, but it is tedious because that means that every transaction you add must be verified.

It's not possible to add data to a block without consensus from the network that the new block is valid and has been verified as a legitimate part of the chain.

To put it mildly, it would be challenging to change any previously verified data.

Now, let's have a look at how we traditionally store data.

The Old Way To Secure Data

The traditional way to protect data is to lock it behind a very secure security system on one computer and a backup computer.

Only those with access to the system can add, access, or remove data. It all seems secure, doesn't it? Well, it is, and it isn't. First, the firewalls put in place do a decent job of protecting the data.

The problem is that the data is stored all in one place. So, your would-be hacker just needs to gain access to the primary server, and then they can do whatever they like.

They can steal information, or initiate legitimate looking financial transfers. And, because they are generating the requests from inside the company's servers, these fake requests can easily be approved.

They can wreak havoc with the system and even go as far as to lock out the authorized users within the company. They can then hold the company to ransom to regain access to their own system. You would have little choice but to pay them – it would be a case of pay up or risk losing all your financial data.

And it's not just unauthorized access that you should be wary of, staff members can also access the system and do damage. What if you had an employee who had a grudge against the company and decided to do damage to the computers internally?

Or what if some crime syndicate approached the company and offered to pay the employee money for client details or other sensitive information? While we like to think that our employees are loyal, criminals can be very persuasive.

So, maybe that centralized system with all the firewall protection is not as secure as we would like to think. And, the Equifax breach that happened in May or June of 2017 seems to bear that out. I say May or June because not even Equifax knows exactly when the breach occurred.

According to CNN, when the story broke in September[2], around about 143 million people may have been affected. And that is a lot of information that might have made it into the wrong hands.

That is a severe breach, and, considering that the company only learned of the breach at the end of July, it's abundantly clear that current safety measures are not adequate.

Captain Blockchain To Save The Day

And here, like some masked superhero comes blockchain to save the day. Why masked? Because, quite simply, blockchain is something that can be difficult to understand and is something that not so many people know about.

Why a superhero? Because it can be a great crime prevention tool. It can help to keep your data completely safe.

---

[2] http://money.cnn.com/2017/09/07/technology/business/equifax-data-breach/index.html

What Makes Blockchain Secure?

- **The database is distributed across different computers**: Every person that is using the blockchain can access the whole database as well as the history thereof. Control, therefore, no longer rests with a single party. The parties to the transaction, thus, do not need to go through an intermediary to verify the data and this can make transfers quicker and less expensive.

- **Transmission from peer-to-peer**: The communication is direct peer-to-peer communication. This is preferable to it having to go through a single, designated node because hackers can and do try to hack the data when it is being transferred through the node. With blockchain, the data is forwarded to all computers within each node. This makes hacking more difficult because the information is not being routed through a single server anymore.

- **Transparency with some anonymity**: You will be able to see which user initiated any data block in the chain and which users verified it. Each node is assigned a unique address as an identifier. You can choose to share your real identity to other people using the chain or choose to remain anonymous. The key here is that this can be anonymous. Your private details are not splashed across the net unless you want them to be. It is possible to track users down through their unique identifiers but is not easily done by the average user.

- **The records are permanent**: Each single transaction is linked to the one that came before it and then the one that came after it. This means that transactions are stored in chronological order. Each transaction is also time-stamped. You cannot change a transaction because that would mean having to replace all the others in the same chain as well. Not only would you need to convince the others on the network to approve the change, but everyone would be able to see that you were the one that made the change in the first place.

- **Computational Logic**: Each transaction can be tied in using computational logic. What this means is that they can be programmed. You could, for example, create an algorithm that would automatically trigger a transaction at a certain point. You could automate processes to be added to the blockchain. They would still need to be verified, but the process from your side could be automated.

Key Takeaways For This Chapter

- The information in a blockchain is stored in blocks, or chunks of data.

- Each block is time-stamped and labeled with the unique identifier of the person adding the data.

- Each block is affixed to a previous block within the network so making changes or deleting a block is difficult. It would mean cutting all the blocks after the block to be altered, rewriting the string, and then getting the other nodes to reauthorize it.

- The blockchain is more secure because the data is spread over many different nodes in the network.

- Centralizing data makes it easier and more tempting for hackers to attack it.

- Each addition or change made to the blockchain must undergo a verification process. The consensus amongst most of the nodes is necessary for transactions to be approved.

In Chapter 2, we'll look a closer look at how blockchain works. You will learn more about the transaction process as well.

Chapter 2: How The Blockchain Works

This chapter is about explaining how blockchain works in a simple and clear manner.

Where Blockchain really shines in the protection of data is that not one person controls all the data. There is also not just one person checking the data either. Contributors add the data and create a new "block" that needs to be checked.

The data is uploaded for verification by multiple users and only actually added to the chain once it is verified. Each person checks the data entered to see that it makes sense and that it is a legitimate addition.

So yes, someone wanting to commit fraud could add something into the blockchain verification queue. However, they would need to be able to convince several checkers from all over the world to allow the fraud to be carried out. The chances of them being able to do this are very slim.

Secondly, as the data is stored in a block and the chain is dispersed over several different computer nodes, the system is difficult to hack. You would need to hack all the computers that the chain is stored on and then change each entry in the whole chain.

Think of blockchain like building a high-rise building. They start off by setting the foundation. This is like the first block in the chain. When the foundation is considered sturdy enough, they build the walls, brick by brick.

The building supervisor and building inspectors will come around to check that the work is proceeding as planned periodically. If a piece of wall is not sound, they'll have to repair or replace it.

If any of the builders decide that they want to make a change and add another window, for example, they will need to get the other builders and architect to check that their plan is sound and agree before it is put in place permanently.

There will be some different people that are involved in building the high rise – builders, plumbers, electricians, roof-layers, etc. so you have a lot more people overseeing the construction.

If they get as far as the sixth floor and decide to change the footprint of the building, for any reason, they'll battle because everything has already been put into place.

Blockchain also uses a series of makers and checkers with diverse backgrounds and different skill sets. No one person can add anything without the consensus of the others.

Also, every single transaction is date-stamped and linked to the IP addresses of both those who input the data and those who checked it. So, if something does go wrong, each inputter and checker is traceable.

Each person within the system does their part and are thus able to create a full transaction within the blockchain. Each verified transaction is timestamped and added to the chain.

It is linked to the block immediately preceding it. The next transaction follows the same process. So, in time, all blocks except the Genesis (or first) block, are linked to the block preceding them. All blocks, except the final block in the sequence, will also be linked to the block that comes directly after them.

The data itself is shared amongst all the nodes, or computers, within the system. Thus, if one computer is hacked or destroyed, the information is still safe anyway.

There are two options when it comes to a blockchain network – public and private networks.

Public Networks

This is where anyone can access or use the system. Examples of public networks include Bitcoin and Ethereum.

Private Networks

One thing that works in the blockchain's favor is that it allows for transparency. You can view the full history of that particular chain. This can be problematic, however, when it comes to sensitive information, like your client's details.

What company would want all their client details accessible to anyone and everyone? The solution is to create a private network by restricting access to the blockchain itself.

Submit Your Data

Whether you are using a public or private network, you need first to add the information. This can be done simply, by writing a line of code, for example.

It's not hard to submit information to the blockchain, but it will need to be verified before it becomes a permanent part of the chain.

Data Is Verified Before Being Added

The data is submitted to the other computers, or nodes, within the network. The other computers will run specialized algorithms to figure out if these changes are legitimate or not, based on what has previously been done in that blockchain.

The final decision as to whether the changes are deemed legitimate or not depends on the consensus of at least 51% of the nodes within the network.

If the network determines that the changes are out of the ordinary for the chain, or that the source of the data is questionable, the information will not be added to it.

So, a hacker could try to add whatever information they want to. The security of the system is in the verification process.

When new data or changes are submitted, the following will be checked before the data is added:

Consensus

This means that most of the nodes in the chain must agree that it was submitted and did happen. So, for example, if you submit that the moon was purple on the 9th of January, most of the nodes in the chain would have to agree before this "fact" is recorded and saved to the chain.

Consistency

The information being added should logically follow on from the previous information in the blockchain. So, going back to our example of the moon being purple on the 9th of January, if the blockchain were used to document phases of the moon, this would be a logical addition.

If on the other hand, the blockchain was being used as a ledger for the property, your submission would be deemed inconsistent.

Transaction

The nodes will also confirm that the actual data submitted is unique and that nothing already within in this chain contradicts the information to be added.

So, retaking the moon example, if someone had previously submitted that the moon was silver on the 9th of January, this would directly contradict the information that you have added, and so the information would not be considered correct or verified.

Automated Conflict Identifiers

The blockchain can monitor itself to help find potential conflicts that exist in the structure itself.

This would be useful for a company that wants to reduce costs associated with security inside the business.

There would be no need to work out complex processes to verify transactions or to have extra security monitoring processes in place. You would rely on the network to authorize transactions.

The company would be able to keep track of all the transactions within the network quite easily.

An Example Of A Cryptocurrency Exchange

Another practical example here is a Bitcoin transaction. Let's say that I am buying something from you for two Bitcoins. I would go into the Bitcoin blockchain and say that I am sending you two Bitcoins.

This information would be submitted to the network. First off, there are a few things that you need to know about Bitcoin - all the Bitcoin transactions since the start are recorded within the network so that the balances can be seen. While our names are not publicly available, the network would be able to identify how many Bitcoins I must have to make sure that I have enough to pay them over to you.

If I have two Bitcoins, the system goes into the next stage of verification, making sure that I am the rightful owner of the Bitcoin account and that the transaction is a legitimate one.

If most of the miners(those who verify Bitcoin transactions) in the system verify the transaction, your Bitcoin balance will increase by two and mine would decrease accordingly.

Now, let's say that I was a fraudster and that I had no actual Bitcoins. The transaction would get no further than the initial check because the miners would be able to verify quickly that I have no Bitcoins to send.

Also, the Bitcoins are not available to be used by you until the first transaction has been verified. So, even though I have recorded that I am sending you the Bitcoins, the transfer has not officially taken place yet.

That means that, if you wanted to pay one of those Bitcoins to someone else at this stage, and submitted that transaction to the blockchain, it would be rejected because the coins weren't reflecting in your account yet.

Key Takeaways For This Chapter

- Blockchains can either be private or public.

- Data is submitted for verification. It is checked for consistency and integrity. It is also checked to ensure that it doesn't conflict with previously recorded data.

- The verification process means that there is always going to be a time lag between the submission of the data and the final addition of it to the blockchain.

In the next chapter, we'll have a look at the history of the blockchain and Bitcoin.

Chapter 3: The History Of The Blockchain & Bitcoin

Where did it all start? Who initially came up with the concept of blockchain and Bitcoin? In this chapter, we will answer those questions.

Satoshi Nakamoto is the name of the man credited with creating the first blockchain and coming up with the idea for the Bitcoin cryptocurrency. However, this is a pseudonym aimed at protecting his/ her real identity.

In fact, no one knows who Satoshi Nakamoto really is, and this has been the source of some lively debate over the years. Some people say that Satoshi lives in Japan, others that he is European. Others still think he is from the United States.

Does it matter that much, though? I don't think so – it makes an interesting debate when you and your friends have a bit of time to spare, but it is not really all that important.

What is important is that the blockchain is not as new a concept as you might think. The first incarnation of the blockchain was developed in 2008 as a backbone for the Bitcoin cryptocurrency.

It was only in 2009, though, that the blockchain was first made public. There was, and still is, a lot of confusion surrounding blockchain and Bitcoin with many people believing that the terms are interchangeable.

The blockchain, however, can operate entirely independently of Bitcoin and is being used by other cryptocurrencies as well. The concept was quickly applied to many other different applications and, by, 2014; it was being used by over eighty other applications as well.

In 2014, Blockchain 2.0 was released. The focus here was more on creating a differentiation between Bitcoin and Blockchain and to define their roles more fully. The changes were to make it clearer that Blockchain is infrastructural, while Bitcoin is an asset.

To make it easier to understand, Bitcoin is just one application that Blockchain can be applied to. The Blockchain makes it possible to keep track of the number of Bitcoins available, who owns what, etc.

The idea was further developed so that it could be more easily scaled and so that more features could be added. The aim was to create an even more functional version. In early 2014, there were at least eight projects in development that used the basic concept as a means for distribution.

If we look at Blockchain today, it has become even more popular. While skeptics initially described it as a flash in the pan idea that would never gain traction, Blockchain is now recognized as a massive disruptor in the security of information industry.

It has even been used by the Russian government to keep their security depository secure.

2015 saw the introduction of Ethereum. This is a software platform that is entirely decentralized and open-ended. It is now the most well-established and largest application of its sort and can be considered an advancement of Blockchain technology.

Ethereum has enabled the development of Distributed Applications (Applications delivered directly to the end user) and SmartContracts (Allowing peer-to-peer contracts.)

The significant advantage of Ethereum over traditional methods is that there is no need to involve a third party in the drafting of contracts. Ethereum is also a specialized programming language rather than just a simple platform.

One thing that is sure is that Blockchain has completely changed the way we look at internet security. The potential is huge.

Key Takeaways For This Chapter

- The concept of the blockchain has been around for a long time.

- The first public application to use blockchain was Bitcoin in 2009.

- Increasingly more apps are being developed using blockchain technology. Ethereum is a more advanced application of the technology with programming language built into it.

- Ethereum offers smart contracts and decentralized apps.

With some knowledge about the history of the blockchain under your belt, it is time to move on to what the advantages of the technology are.

Chapter 4: The Advantages Of Blockchain Technology

What is wonderful about the blockchain? In this chapter, we'll explore that.

The real value of the Blockchain is that it makes it possible for the sharing of a database without the need for one specific administrator. It makes true disintermediation a reality.

This is helpful because a database is a tangible thing. It might be present in the form of characters on a computer, but a database is something that has value. If its contents are controlled by centralized authority, such as a government or bank, it is possible for the database to be tampered with or corrupted.

The hacking of Experian was a perfect example of why disintermediation makes sense. If Experian had made use of Blockchain technology, the information would have been a lot safer.

Disintermediation adds a layer of security that is simply not attainable in any other way. While the data can be changed quite easily when a single server is involved, data spread across several nodes, as is the case with blockchain, is a lot more resistant to tampering.

The security of the information is not the only thing that is being protected, the integrity of the information is as well. Let's say, for example, that a government organization wanted to go in and change data as a part of a cover-up. With a centralized computer system, this becomes a whole lot easier.

With the blockchain, however, it becomes much harder, if not impossible, to erase transactions recorded originally.

The system also helps to reduce the chances of human error. With the ability to automate many of the processes within the blockchain, and the cryptography securing the information, there are fewer chances for human error to creep in.

Greater Empowerment

Because the users control both the information and the transactions, without the need for third-party involvement, they are more empowered.

You get to decide the rules for your transactions, not some third-party. While the transactions are verified, they are not subject to the arbitrary rules that an intermediary might impose.

A Better Quality Of Data

Blockchain data is accurate, widely available and of consistently high quality.

Increased Reliability

Because the network is reliant on several nodes rather than a single server, it tends to be more reliable. Even if 80% or 90% of the nodes within the system went down, the others would still be able to function, and the information stored within the blockchain would remain intact.

Say goodbye to server downtime.

Longer-Lasting

Again, because the system relies on several nodes and not a single server, it can outlast a traditional network. If the server is taken down, a traditional network is finished. With the blockchain, the information will still be available even if several computers within the network are down.

Transparency

If a public blockchain is changed, everyone can see the changes that have been made meaning that nothing can be hidden within the blockchain.

Permanency

Once transactions have been added, they cannot be easily changed or deleted. The chain becomes a permanent record.

Simplification

A central ledger makes things a lot simpler. There is no unnecessary clutter.

Transaction Speed Improved

While there is some time delay in getting the transactions added to the blockchain, this is still faster than is the case in some traditional systems. Take a financial transaction, for example.

If moving money traditionally from bank A to bank B, the transaction must first be checked and authorized internally by bank A and then passed onto a clearinghouse before being transferred to bank B. It must then be checked and authorized by someone at bank B as well, before being paid into your account.

This is not a quick process, and it can be slowed down even more if there is a public holiday or weekend while the verification is being done. The transaction is done during business hours when the bank is open for business. If the bank is closed, the transaction will halt.

With blockchain, the transactions are faster because they are done directly and can be processed at any time. If you are sitting up at one o'clock in the morning, and your Bitcoins are burning a hole in your pocket, you can fund a transaction.

Because the miners come from all around the world, they will be available at all sorts of various times of day to verify the transaction.

Cheaper Transactions

The costs are lower because the computing power required to run the system is divided amongst users. And the fact that the verification process is simpler means that the costs for security, etc. are lower as well.

Different Applications

The system can be used in various applications. For example, you could use it to create a ledger for property ownership. You could also use it to facilitate financial transactions.

It could be used in healthcare as well to allow better access to patient healthcare records. Digital signatures could be utilized to ensure that only those authorized to do so could view your health records.

Let's examine how this could work in practice. You could go to your doctor's office for a general checkup. In the past, that information would have been updated in your file and kept with the doctor's office where only your doctor would have access to it.

If you changed doctors, you would have to have your file transferred. If you had to be admitted to hospital in an emergency, the hospital would be able to contact your doctor, if they had your doctor's details and were able to get hold of them. The hospital would create a new file for you on their own system.

There would be no real record-sharing between the two.

With the blockchain, however, your doctor would update the details of tests performed, diagnoses, and medicine prescribed by the system. If you went to another doctor, that doctor would simply need to input your details and find your file. They would then update the blockchain file.

If you were admitted to the hospital, the same would happen. Each different service provider would record their information in the same place, and this would enable you to have a complete picture when it came to your health issues.

It would also enable them to access relevant information timeously and will allow them to avoid the duplication of tests.

But things could be taken a step further as well. The insurance companies could also link into the system, making the payment of medical claims faster, less expensive and less vulnerable to fraud.

Blockchain could also be used to secure computer systems and firmware within the defense system as well. This would make it harder for hackers to gain access to the system and, at the same time, make it more difficult for them to take critical systems offline.

In general, government services could be improved by allowing the easier exchange of information between different departments. The verification part of the process and transparency of information stored in a blockchain system could be useful in preventing corruption.

The legal system is already benefiting from the use of blockchain technology. Blockchains can contain copious quantities of data securely. "Smart contracts" are protocols that allow the facilitation and enforcement of contracts.

Contracts can be put in place on the system without the need to refer the matter to an intermediary. Funds can be placed in escrow and paid out only as predetermined milestones have been achieved – protecting both parties to the contract.

An Open-Source System

The blockchain is entirely open-source. This means that anyone can tinker it in accordance to their needs. This fosters creativity and allows for further advances to be made because developers have the source code easily accessible.

That and the fact that the system is reliable and decentralized have already been benefitting developers of applications. Who knows what they will be able to come up with in future as a result?

That about wraps up the benefits of the blockchain. Concisely, these include increased security, increased reliability, more empowerment for users, higher quality data, transparency, and permanency, lower costs and reduced transaction speeds.

Key Takeaways for This Chapter Are

The advantages of blockchain include:

- Greater empowerment

- A better quality of data

- Increased reliability

- More permanency

- Transparency

- A simplification of processes

- Cheaper transaction costs

- Different applications for the technology

- Open-source code

The technology sounds great but before we all jump on the blockchain bandwagon, let's have a look what the disadvantages of the system are.

Chapter 5: The Disadvantages Of Blockchain Technology

Okay, blockchain sounds great. So why hasn't it been more widely adopted? The blockchain is good, but it's not perfect. And, to be frank, some of the issues are serious. In this chapter, we will examine those issues.

It's Not That Easy To Understand

For proponents of the blockchain system, this is not a popular sentiment, but it is, unfortunately, a true one. The blockchain is a difficult concept to understand for most people as it is and there isn't enough useful information out there to change this at the moment.

You would need to educate people about what the blockchain is, and how they can use it. And that is not going to be easy because it really is a concept that is different to how most people think.

And, if you don't understand how it works, there is a good chance that you will end up feeling frustrated using the blockchain. How willing would you be to adopt a system that you felt wasn't working for you?

The system is not very easy to use. You do need to be computer-savvy to use the system.

That brings up another point; there is an idea out there that blockchain and Bitcoin are reserved for those who are brilliant with computers. Anyone can learn how to use it if they put in a little effort.

And, while the anonymity of users is a plus, the unique identifier is not always that easy to get a handle on. Take your Bitcoin wallet ID, for example. It consists of a string of randomly generated alpha and numeric characters and is very long.

You don't get to choose your own Bitcoin wallet name and, at 36 characters, it can be tough to remember.

Searching a blockchain for something specific is not easy. It's not like Google where you can just type in the search phrase you want to find.

There May Be Negative Associations Made

There was a lot of bad press about Bitcoins being used as a form of currency to pay for illicit activities on the dark web. People have not forgotten this, and it is hard to change that association.

The tide is turning with there being a lot of positive articles about the technology, but the negative associations are still there for now.

The Infrastructure Is Not There

Partly because of the lack of understanding about what the blockchain is, and partly because of the small chance of reward for mining Bitcoins, there are not enough people adopting the system and creating nodes. This prevents the system being implemented it on a vast scale.

Having a few hundred-people added here, and there is not a problem, but what would happen if you started to add hundreds of thousands?

This system at this stage just doesn't have enough capacity to handle a lot of people being added to the system. The more transactions that are being put through the system, the more computing power is needed and, so, more nodes are needed to meet this demand.

The Verification Process Is Too Long

Now, the average financial transaction on the blockchain could take 15 minutes to verify. This is not a lot of time when compared to traditional transfers between banks and is a lot faster than a bank to bank transfer. We have already established that. It is also not a problem as long as the transaction is not time-sensitive.

But when it comes to things like stock trading, it can become a real issue. Ten minutes can be a lifetime when it comes to the buying and selling of shares. The price could increase and decrease several times over. For stock traders, the lags in the system at present would be very off-putting.

It's not just time-sensitive financial transactions that could be problematic, though. Self-driving cars are not widely available now, but that could change in future. If the car needed to adjust its course to avoid a collision, how easily would it be able to do that if there was a time lag in the verification process?

The Records Are Permanent

Permanent records can be a good thing and a bad thing. If you bought a house, for example, you'd want a permanent record of the transaction.

But what if you defaulted on your mortgage payment and your house got repossessed? With the way that credit records work today, you would be applying to have the record expunged if you pay the debt or you could wait for it to fall away on its own. (Depending on the type of default or judgment, this could after five years after being listed.)

With the blockchain, however, it would be there forever. Every creditor that viewed your credit history would be able to see it. This could affect your chances of getting credit in future, and it could have a negative influence when it came to the cost of credit granted to you.

The higher the risk you pose to the lender, the more the credit is going to cost you. They would charge you higher interest rates and would be able to justify having done so.

Having a permanent record, in this case, is not a positive thing.

Also, it may also influence your chances of getting a job because many job applicants are put through a credit screening process when they apply as well.

It is scary to think that a mistake that you made could end up haunting you for the rest of your life in this way.

It Is Very Energy Intensive

The cost regarding energy usage can be staggering. The effect of running all those different verifications equates to a much higher charge in energy.

It was estimated that managing the system for Bitcoin in 2015 cost around $100 million in energy costs. Considering the small amount of money being protected at the time, in the region of only $3 billion, that is a substantial cost.

While the cost is spread amongst the different users in the system, that's a lot by any standard. If the bigger banks and governments got involved as well, or the number of users increased, you would have millions more transactions to verify.

The financial cost of all that electricity being consumed is bad enough, but the environmental cost would be even worse. With most people working to reduce their carbon footprints, this extensive energy usage could pose a fundamental problem in the large-scale adoption of the technology.

It's not all doom and gloom, though. The current banks of server farms do also require a lot of energy to maintain. They need to have specialized cooling systems to prevent the servers from overheating.

Hopefully, with the development of new, more energy efficient computers and the development of alternative energy sources, this will have a much smaller impact in future.

There Are Legalities That Must Be Addressed

The laws will need to be changed to discuss legal issues that might crop up, especially as far as the transfer of assets is concerned. Say, for example, there is a dispute over property ownership, how would that be decided?

Are there even laws governing these kinds of online contracts? Is there recourse to the courts if something goes wrong?

It stands to reason that there will need to be some regulation in future if these systems are to be more widely adopted. And that goes against the ideals on which blockchain was based in the first place.

There is also the question of how well the system will be regulated. With the current level of understanding of what blockchain is, there is a chance that regulations may be ineffective or incorrectly drafted and badly enforced.

There is also the issue that there are bound to be those who use the technology for illegal transactions. The anonymity of the system could be detrimental in this case.

Bitcoin, as we have discussed, has been used for illegal transactions. People have used the system to pay for things such as human trafficking, murders for hire, terrorism, etc.

How do you legally determine who is committing the crime here? You could argue that the blame would rest with the two parties to the transaction. In the traditional legal system, that would be pretty cut and dried.

But what if the defense argues that those who authorized the transaction are also complicit and should be held accountable? They could argue that because so many others endorsed the action, their client was not entirely to blame for the crime.

A simple money transfer could be made to look like anything. Those authorizing the transactions might do so in complete innocence, without realizing that they were aiding a criminal.

But what about the greyer legal areas? Say, for example, someone molests your child, and you decide that you want to make them pay. You could set up a "reward" within a blockchain system for someone to hurt or kill the person who hurt your child.

Legally speaking, this would be wrong, and we all know that, but many people would feel that you were justified in your actions. So, if someone did punish the guilty party on your behalf, they could apply for the reward, and it might be verified.

The transaction would go through the normal verification process. If consensus was reached and the money paid out, those authorizing the transaction would effectively be complicit in the crime.

How would that case be handled? Would they be liable for prosecution as well? How many of the verifiers would you prosecute? What would legal precedent be set if they were prosecuted? How would you prosecute people in different countries?

This is where the use of the blockchain system might be on slippery ground. The anonymity of the system could become a legal issue.

Automation Of The System Means Fewer Jobs

One concern that has been noted is that businesses will be able to reduce their staff compliments because of this technology. It is a legitimate fear, and it might have some impact on the global economy.

But there is another way to look at this as well. How many jobs will the technology create? Take Bitcoin, for example. Bitcoin mining has become an industry all its own.

Bitcoins can be earned by helping to verify transactions. They were initially offered to create an incentive to get people to verify transactions. In the preliminary stages, this was a way to earn a little bit of extra money, and bitcoin mining became an actual profession.

It was created out of nothing. Nowadays, mining bitcoins is not as simple – you need some serious computing power to be able to work the system, and there is a lot of competition out there, but Bitcoins are worth a lot.

Bitcoins are a type of currency. They can be traded, used to buy things, and even be sold. While the original value of the currency was low, one coin is now worth close to $5000, so they have become an asset that investors look out for as well.

It's a good example though how blockchain can help to create jobs and stimulate the economy. Who knows what similar incentives might be created in future?

At this stage in time, you can't merely say that it is going to cost too many jobs. If you look at the way that so many traditional industries are being changed and new ones created, it becomes clear that change is something that can be an excellent thing for the economy.

Look at the development of non-traditional industries like Airbnb and Uber, for example. They have created a whole new income source for many people. Twenty years ago, no one would even have thought of either of these types of business models. Who knows what we'll come up with in future?

You could also look at the Ethereum system and the Dapps capability. This makes it easier and less expensive to get apps to the market, and this creates another type of industry.

Not Enough Nodes

Every transaction on the blockchain system needs to be verified. This takes time, computing power and some effort. For people to commit their resources, it must be worth their while.

They need to be getting some kind reward from the entire process. Currently, for example, you could try to mine Bitcoins. But, unless you have the right equipment, being successful at mining Bitcoins is not that easy.

Other systems, such as Ethereum also allow miners to earn Ethers analogously but it always comes down to factoring whether the increased costs of allowing the system to run on your computer are worth the rewards you are earning.

If the costs outweigh the benefits of being a part of a blockchain network, how many people would want to join? Without new members, it is not possible to grow the network at all.

You also have to deal with the issue that miners could leave. And that is a genuine concern here. What if something new comes along, something that offers a better chance of making money? What happens if your network starts to decrease instead of expanding?

As we have mentioned before, even with 90% of the nodes down, the system could still function. But how long would it take to get new transactions verified? And would the system be able to handle all the transactions or would it crash?

This Could Be Regarded As Big Business

There is a lot of buzz about the blockchain system. What happens if a large corporate company decided that they could make money off the system?

It's difficult to rewrite bits of the blockchain but not impossible. If you have enough money, you could hire someone to rewrite what you like. You could also pay to get all the changes verified by enough people in the chain.

Currently, the expense would not be worth the reward but what if a way was found to monetize the system?

There Are Inherent Dangers

Blockchains are much more secure than traditional systems. Now, hacking the system is not worth the effort. What if it becomes more widely adopted and used to store more digital assets and information? If it became worthwhile to do, hackers might start looking for an alternative way to break in.

You could have thieves hacking into your home security system and shutting it down so they could more easily break in. This is something that, though difficult to do, could be possible and it is something that needs to be addressed.

Currently, the consensus is that blockchain is not hackable. Is this attitude going to mean that people are not going to work on securing it more?

The Is No General Administrator

This is good goof for the autonomy of a system but can stunt its development overall.

Without a unified vision of what steps to take, how do you move forward? This has already been seen to affect blockchain.

So many people have opinions on how to move forward with blockchain, and they can't seem to agree. And some general direction is necessary here.

How do we make sure that blockchain apps are sustainable? Take Bitcoins, for example, what happens when they do run out? (There was a finite number created, and that is one of the reasons that they are becoming much harder to find now.)

What do you do to get new people to join? How do you get the current members to stay on board?

Performance

This can be a problem going forward; the system is never going to be as quick as a centralized system would be. It's just not possible because the blockchain requires more work to be done.

To start off with, each transaction must be assigned a digital signature. This can be done through a system like ECDSA. It is essential because there will be no other way of proving what the source of the transaction is otherwise.

While you can group a few different payments under the same transaction, it is still necessary for the system to verify each new request that you try to add to the blockchain. On a centralized database, you simply need to verify your identity once, and then you can transact as normal. Each new request does not need further verification.

The process of reaching a consensus within the blockchain does take time. And, depending on the mechanism used, this can involve a lot of communicating with the person submitting the transactions and the people that are verifying them.

Redundancy is another issue that could cause delays. On a centralized system, your transaction would only need to be entered one time. On a blockchain network, each node in the related network will need to process the transactions. This means that a lot of extra work will need to be done.

While there are quite a few kinks in the system to work out, these are by no means insurmountable. As the blockchain technology becomes better understood and more utilized, more people will start to work on finding solutions for these issues.

Key Takeaways For This Chapter

The disadvantages of blockchain include:

- It is hard to understand

- There are negative associations with the dark web

- We don't have the infrastructure yet

- Verification takes too long in some instances

- The records are never deleted

- It uses a lot of electricity

- The laws surrounding it need to be revised

- Jobs could be lost because of greater use of the technology

- There are not enough people verifying the data

- Complacency about the security of the system could mean that new security measures are not developed timeously

- There is no one governing body to steer the development of the blockchain

- Performance will always be an issue because the nature of the system means that there is a lot of redundancy built into it.

Now that you understand the disadvantages of the blockchain system, it's time to move forward and look at how Blockchain has impacted the financial services industry.

Chapter 6: Blockchain's Impact On The Finance Industry

Cryptography is the standard way for us to secure our online financial transactions. The problem with this system is that there are so many different intermediaries necessary to the process. This increases the chances of leaks in the security.

When you buy something online, for example, you must give over all your credit card details. This may be risky, especially if you are not sure who you are dealing with.

You enter your details, and a third party processes the transaction. You should trust that the site that you are buying from is legitimate and that it has adequate encryption software in place to prevent hackers from accessing your card details.

Also, all your details are transmitted to the third party processing the transaction. It's a lot of information weaving its way around the web.

Cryptocurrencies were developed as a way around this. They make it possible to pay for transactions without the need to disclose your personal details to anyone.

They are completely changing the face of the financial industry because you don't even need to use a bank account or card to make purchases. All you do is to buy the cryptocurrency and then transfer it over to the seller.

There is no need to worry about whether your credit card details are secure during the transaction because you just don't use them.

Another area in which blockchain is turning the financial services industry on its head is in the way the money is transferred. Traditionally, when paying someone, there are three parties to the transaction – your bank, a company that processes the payment and their bank.

With cryptocurrencies, you just send the money straight to the person directly. There are no banks involved. This makes transaction fees a lot less expensive simply because it is cutting out all the intermediaries that would typically profit from the transaction.

Also, because blockchain is open-sourced, new apps could be developed that further change the financial services industry.

It's also not a case of if the blockchain is going to adopted by the financial services industry, it's now a case of when. Some of the big names in the industry have already started considering it.

They are leveraging the potential of the chain to allow them to increase the speed at which transactions are processed, how secure their databases are and as a way of cutting costs and passing these savings on to the consumer.

The potential range of applications that might be developed is staggering, and it can truly be said that blockchain will transform some different online applications in future.

Some applications have been developed to work with cryptocurrencies and those that have been developed to work without them as well.

It is more likely that those using cryptocurrency will win the day when it comes to real changes in the financial services industry.

Another thing that makes Bitcoin so different is that it is a global ledger and can be accessed anywhere. Now, take your standard banking model. If you are traveling abroad, you may need to inform your bank ahead of time so that your card would work abroad.

Every time you used that card, you'd be liable to pay a whole bunch of extra charges.

If you were using Bitcoins, on the other hand, all you would need to do would be to log into a computer and send the money through the Bitcoin blockchain.

Of course, while blockchain is a model that is already disrupting the financial services industry, we are not at the point where we can get rid of our bank cards altogether yet.

The time it takes to verify transactions could be a real problem with the point of sale transactions. If it takes at least 10 minutes for the system to authorize one payment, few retail outlets would want to put up with the increase in queuing that this would cause.

If, however, a way could be found to improve the speed of the verification process, I could see us using cryptocurrency to pay for goods in future.

It would be safer for both the merchant and us. We would not have to hand over a card with all our details on it, so this could be a way to cut back on cloning of cards.

Merchants would benefit because the money would be in their account within minutes. Currently, with the normal point of sale transactions, this can take a few days.

And there is always some recourse in the case of a dispute when transactions are processed through the blockchain. Because transactions are permanently recorded, you would be able to go back and see the transaction in question, even months later.

Think what this could mean for product returns, as an example – you would not need to keep the till slip because the information would be easily accessible in the blockchain.

A lot of concern has been raised over how safe the blockchain system is. Is it a good idea to entrust a system that is spread over so many nodes?

First off, the blockchain is protected by an extremely powerful encryption. That, the anonymity of the users and the verification process make it difficult to commit fraud.

You have the added benefit of knowing that there are no actual "staff" members working within the chain. This means that you don't have to worry about a staff member either making use of your details or selling off your personal information.

It works on a similar principle to when you walk into your bank and fetch your safety deposit box. You will need to prove your identity to gain access to the box, even if you have the key.

The digital trail that is formed using the blockchain is also a big plus for the financial services industry. Attempts to commit fraud could be picked up as and when they occurred and stopped before they are successful and money is lost.

Blockchain offers us a way to record our transactions and process them in real time. It can be said that this is going to change the face of the financial services industry forever.

Key Takeaways For This Chapter

- Significant players in the financial industry are already considering adopting blockchain technology

- Everyone agrees that blockchain will continue to have a profound impact on how we process financial transactions going forward.

Now that you understand how the blockchain is changing our financial services industries, we can move on to learning how non-financial industries are being disrupted.

Chapter 7: Ethereum, Smart Contracts, And Decentralized Apps

In this chapter, we are going to look at Ethereum, Smart Contracts, and Decentralized Apps.

What Is Ethereum?

This is a platform, based on the blockchain. It is public and open-source. It seems like the blockchain, but it is a lot more – it's like blockchain on steroids.

It allows for the setting up and execution of smart contracts; it will enable developers to create Decentralized apps and offer them direct to the public and it also offers a cryptocurrency.

Why Use Ethereum At All?

Ethereum offers an alternative protocol to use when building apps. The benefits of the system are that development time can be accelerated and that there is a higher level of security for apps that are hardly used or that are small. Ethereum makes it easier for different applications to interact with one another.

Ethereum's base layer is a blockchain that has a Turing-complete programing language built into it. This makes it possible for people to create their own smart contracts easily, with the least amount of knowledge.

There is a very basic version of Namecoin that you can write in just a couple of lines of code. Some of the more advanced protocols, like those for currencies, can be written in less than twenty lines of code. This makes it a lot easier for beginners to use.

Ethereum offers a lot more features that your basic blockchain and, because of the base programming language, it provides a lot more powerful features as well.

What Is Ether?

Ether is the cryptocurrency used within Ethereum. You can mine Ether just like you mine Bitcoins.

Ether is what keeps Ethereum running because it is what is used to pay transaction fees. There are two different sorts of accounts – those that are owned externally and that have private keys and contract accounts that are controlled using their code.

I don't want to get overly technical here so let's explain it simply. An external account is something that you use to send messages. You do this by creating a new transaction and digitally signing it.

A contract account works differently. You set up the coded contract ahead of time, and when a message is sent to this contract account, the code is activated. The system will the act in a predetermined manner.

So, let's say, for example, I am doing some construction work for you. We set up progress payments along the way so that when we are halfway through, for example, I receive a payment.

You put the funds in escrow, and I get to work. When I get halfway through, some of the funds are to be released. The contract will then do the requisite work, and I will get my funds.

Can You Mine Ethereum?

So, if Ethereum is like blockchain on steroids, does that mean you can mine Ether the same way you would do with Bitcoins on blockchain? Ethereum is different from blockchain.

But, a quick answer to that question is that yes, you can mine for Ether.

What Is Mining In This Sense?

I'll never forget a friend of mine who owned a very successful coffee shop. He was constantly told how he had a real gold mine there. And he agreed because he would say, "Yes, a gold mine is a heck of a lot of work."

Mining on Ethereum is also a lot of work. Forget this idea that you are going to become rich overnight – to mine fast enough to make a significant amount of money, you will need a great computer system, and that doesn't come cheap.

You also are not the only one that is going to be looking.

What happens during mining is that you are taking part in the system. You are helping provide the answers to mathematics problems that can be challenging. These problems are so complex that you need to use a lot of computing power to solve them.

Basically, what you will do is to use your computer's processing power with a set of mining applications.

The information that comprises each transaction must be encoded into data blocks. These blocks link to other blocks to form a blockchain. We knew this already. Here's the kicker, to keep the transactions running smoothly, each of the blocks must be analyzed as fast as possible.

To maintain a network that would be able to do this efficiently would mean spending a lot of money. What Ethereum and Bitcoin do instead is to offer incentives for people to come in and help them with this process.

The miner will spend time, processing power, space on their computer and power to sort the blocks. They do this so that they can find the right solution and then submit this to the system. The person who is issuing the cryptocurrency, in this case, Ether, will offer rewards based on the information that was verified. The miners will usually also be able to earn digital coins.

By mining, miners are both helping to improve the security of the network, verifying transactions, and increasing the speed at which the transactions can be processed.

Developers using the Ethereum network and those initiating smart contracts will need to pay Ether to proceed. As a miner, you can keep your Ether, use it to buy goods from those who will accept it or sell it outright.

The value of the Ether will depend on the demand for it. The higher the demand, the higher the price you can get.

Like Bitcoins, there is not an endless supply of Ether. There is only 18 million Ether issued on an annual basis. Ethereum did say that this could change at some stage, though.

Every developer seeking to engage and make use of smart contracts on the Ethereum blockchain needs Ether to proceed. It is popularly called the fuel that runs Ethereum. It is a less expensive way of running transactions on a traditional network.

You can sell or trade your Ether after mining it.

What Are Smart Contracts?

Smart contracts are contracts that have been converted to computer code. They are then uploaded to the blockchain. The system would handle ensuring that monies are paid out, etc.

If you have something of value that you want to sell, you have a few options. You can use a middleman, such as a lawyer, to ensure that the exchange is done fairly. This is going to cost you money. You could trust that the other person will do their part and avoid the middleman. This will save you money but what happens if the other party turns out not to be trustworthy? A smart contract is another alternative.

Smart contracts allow you to set up an exchange without the need for a middleman.

It's like going to a vending machine to buy soda. You put the money in, and the machine checks your money and if everything is correct spits out your soda. If it isn't, it gives the money back.

With a smart contract, you'll need to use a cryptocurrency, but the system is basically the same.

You and the buyer would determine the terms. They would set up the smart contract and pay the funds in. The funds will be held in escrow until the transaction is done. The buyer will provide their identity, address, etc. whatever they need so that you can get the goods to them.

They can also specify a date by which the goods need to be delivered, etc. and can also enforce penalties if you are late. The system will automatically act on the terms of the contract.

When the agreed step is complete, payment will be made. So basically, the system centers on the "If then" principle.

The Advantages of Smart Contracts

There are a lot of pluses with smart contracts.

- **It's on your terms:** You set out the terms of the contract as you want them. There is no need for legal jargon that you really don't need.

- **You are on your own**: But in a good way. No third party might want to influence the agreement in any way. You don't have to wait for a third party to process the agreement – the system will execute it automatically.

- **It's backed up**: On the blockchain, the document is duplicated many times over. You only need one copy, but you'll have several backups. Neither party can "lose" the original.

- **Trust**: Everything is digitally signed and, if necessary, funds are placed in escrow. You don't need to trust that the other person will keep up to their end. The "documents" are digitally signed so there is no way to say they have been misunderstood.

- **The contract is safe**: The likelihood of a hacker being able to crack the encryption are minimal. They also would not be able to do anything with the funds in escrow as these can only be paid out regarding the contract. If anyone tries to change the contract, all parties are notified.

- **It is a faster way of doing things**: It's as simple as filling in a form. You don't need to write out reams and reams of paperwork as most of the basic work is done for you in the coding.

- **You save money**: You don't have to pay someone to draw up the contract, you don't have to pay to have it witnessed by a notary.

- **Accuracy**: The contract is simple, and there is less chance of you making an error. The computer handles the execution, and this also reduces the chances of making a serious error.

The Disadvantages of Smart Contracts

Some things still need to be worked on.

- **Bugs**: What if a bug works its way into the code? That could prevent it being executed or send the money to the wrong account.

- **Regulation**: How is any authority going to regulate these contracts. How will the tax be determined on them?

- **No way to rescind the contract**: These contracts are set up and will execute automatically. What happens if the item I send out is a fake or broken? The funds are going to be released to me on proof of delivery, and the system will do that. There is no way to stop it from doing so.

Dapps Based on Ethereum That Have Been Successful

- **Golem:** The idea was simple – to create a global market where users could sell idle computer power. Golem boasts a market cap in the region of $220 million and is set to release its initial version, named Brass Golem early next year. The initial phase is set to test how well Golem will be able to handle CGI rendering. If this turns out to be successful and sustainable, Golem will make it possible for those creating CGI images to rent resources from users with idle computer power to make rendering much faster. The idle computer would be able to accept multiple tasks. This is quite exciting because it could end up making access to pooled resources available to all. It would be like creating a massive supercomputer.

- **Augur:** The idea behind Augur is equally brilliant, and we have spoken a little about it already. It boasts a market cap exceeding $200 million. Now, it is beta tested. It looks set to create a powerful forecasting tool, allowing many to make gains on the m

- **Melonport:** This blockchain-based protocol is aimed at digital asset management (DAM). Those using this app can set up or invest in, DAM strategies competitively and transparently. The blockchain helps to reduce the costs and time necessary for this. Melonport has started something completely unique DAM world in that it helps to build a record of accomplishment that is visible and completely auditable.

- **Status:** This app helps to you access Ethereum from your mobile device, from anywhere you want to. It helps make your smartphone a light client node within the network. This makes it easier to use the messaging system, to send smart contracts and for users to exchange payments as well. Because the app is based on a peer-to-peer network protocol, you don't have to worry about server downtimes.

- **Brave:** This is an ICO that is still in development, but it looks extremely interesting. It is said that around about 60% of the time taken for a website to load is because of the ad technology embedded into it. Brave Browser will be designed to shield your IP address from tracking by third parties. This will enable your browser to load faster. Another feature that they will be introducing is that you can enable ads if you like and you will receive tokens as a result. So, you can also benefit from the ads displayed on websites, or you can choose to turn them off completely.

- **Aragon**: Aragon is also still in development and is extremely ambitious. The aim is to allow you to manage an entire organization on the blockchain platform. This would mean that you no longer must worry about issues like endless paperwork and geographical borders.

These are just some examples of the Dapps that are likely to change the way we do things. The idea here is to come up with completely new and revolutionary ideas that will make life better for everyone. To create useful applications that have real value.

Are You Dapper?

Do you have a brilliant idea for a dapp of your own? While Ethereum is still starting out, there has been growing interest in it because the Ether recently increased in price.

So, if you have a dapp that you want to design, it's an excellent idea to start getting to know Solidity. This is the programming language used within Ethereum to create executable distributed code contracts.

How to Get Your Dapp Off the Ground

- **Write a whitepaper**: Plan what problem that your dapp is going to address. Be extremely clear about what your intention is and what goals you have regarding your dapp. How are you going to go about distributing tokens for your dapp? (This is what people will get in exchange for investing,) Decide on how you will establish consensus and how you are going to find a management and development team to work on the idea. If you foresee technical issues, be upfront about it and make sure that people understand exactly what your technical requirements are.

- **Start to build a following**: Start getting the idea out there, start forming a community around the idea. You'll get valuable feedback and get to gauge potential interest in the idea.

- **Begin a crowd-sale**: When you have drummed up a reasonable amount of interest, you can start a crowd-sale to raise funds. This is where people who want to invest in the idea provide funding in exchange for tokens. Create a decent website and put all the details about your proposed Dapp in place. The website and your whitepaper are what will convince investors to trust you with their money, so make it good.

- **Go into development**: When you have raised enough capital to start, you can get working on the app. You will need to work with a developer who understands what you are after and who will be able to deliver the results that you want.

Finding The Right Developer For Your Dapp

The right developer can help get your project off the ground and make it successful. It is a real investment in your business, so it pays to get this one right.

Here's more detail on what to look for in a dapp developer. It's not only about price – the cheapest option may end up costing you more in the long-run because of delays or the app not working as it should.

- **The developer should have an interest in the business**: The developer is being hired on for a single project, but they should care about your business. They should be rooting for you and wanting you to succeed. If the developer is interested, it will show in their work. They will work on creating the perfect app for and walk you through the process. They will want the app to be as much of a success as you do.

- **Check their previous work**: Any developer worth their salt should have a decent body of work similar to what you want them to work on. Check what their experience is with app development. Take some time to look at the apps they have developed and see how professional they look and how well they run. The work that the developer has done previously gives you a good insight into the level of skill they have and to how detail-orientated they are. Apps are tricky – you need someone who can focus on both the important things and the smaller, less critical aspects of the app. Getting the right results and delivering a superb customer experience should be their main goal.

- **Ask for references**: If they are halfway decent at their job, they should not have a problem giving you references. The references should be related to building apps. Ask the reference what it was like to work with the developer, what worth ethic they had and whether they delivered their work on time.

- **Build a relationship**: You need someone that you get on with. The dapp may need to be tweaked or updated at a later stage. The developer you choose should be willing to help you improve the app based on what the end-users are saying about it.

- **Price is not the only issue**: Price may be a factor, but you need to consider all the other factors as well. As mentioned above, hiring the wrong developer is going to cost you time and money and could put the reputation of your business at risk. If the reviews for your dapp are negative, you are going to battle to get it to a point where it is profitable.

- **Keep an eye on the big picture**: It is important to get a developer who can create the app flawlessly. It is also crucial that the app looks good and professional. You will also need to consider who will test the dapps functionality and design. This can be trickier if you choose a designer running a one-person show.

- **Hey, good looking**: You will need someone to notice your Dapp, stop and examine it and want to buy it. For that to happen, you need to ensure that the app looks great. Think about the features that your end-user will like and how they will go about using the dapp. Keep all the pages looking consistent and flawless.

Your dapp designer is going to oversee creating the dapp of your dreams. Don't fob off this important task on someone else.

What Is An Initial Coin Offering (ICO)?

The introduction of a new dapp on Ethereum or other blockchain-based systems usually entails having an ICO. This is to raise funds through the sale of tokens. This is like stocks in a company except that tokens do not entitle the holder to a say in running the company.

You will determine the value of your token to start off with. The token will then be listed on the exchange. The price will then go up or down, depending on demand for the token within the exchange.

What is important to remember is that the ICO can generate interest in the tokens and bring in much-needed revenue. So, no matter how highly experts value the ICO, do make sure to keep interest peaked with regular updates and make sure that your value proposition is a great one.

Do You Want To Invest In An ICO?

ICOs can be a fantastic way to get in on the ground floor of a company that will hopefully do well, but there are risks involved. It should be considered along the same lines as a venture capital investment.

There is no guarantee that things will work out but you can reduce your risks by doing the following:

- **Keep updated on the details**: Regularly check the website, Twitter account or whatever social media pages they are running. If they have a Slack group, follow that as well. Make sure that you will receive notifications so that you can see when their ICO goes public.

- **Get your wallet**: It is best to stick to a wallet on myetherwallet.com. These wallets will not change address like an exchange wallet can do, and it can accept ICO tokens – not all wallets are. You will need to make sure that you have enough Ether in your wallet and enough to cover the cost of the transactions. If you do not, your transaction will not go through, and you could lose out.

- **Time it perfectly**: If the ICO starts at two o'clock in the morning, be there at 2 o'clock in the morning. The more popular the ICO, the faster it will close. Get everything ready beforehand, so there is no delay when purchasing your ICOs.

- **Keep your tokens safe**: You can transfer the tokens out of your wallet once it has been listed and becomes available on the exchange. You can transfer tokens to the exchange to begin trading them.

Which ICO Do I Choose?

This is like any other investment that you are going to make. You need to consider the following:

- **How safe is the investment?** The higher the risk, the higher the potential for reward but also the higher the chance that you can lose your money. How trustworthy are the developers? How trustworthy is the founder of the company developing the app?

- **How well do they plan:** Does the whitepaper lay out the steps in a clear and logical fashion? Do they have a good business plan in place? What about the development team and the management team? Will they be able to pull this off?

- **Is this good marketing or a good plan?** Some developers will go to the trouble of hiring a good marketer and setting up something that looks great on paper, but that really doesn't hold water. Be careful not to be taken in by a shiny, new website and examine the plan carefully. Do some research into the idea for yourself. Is the problem that they are solving a real one?

- **How do you get out of it?** What happens if you decide you need to leave? At what level will you decide to cut your losses and run, if it comes down to it?

- **What is their unique value proposition?** What is going to make the end-consumer sit up and notice this dapp? What is original about the idea? Has it all been done before? There will be lots of developers coming up with dapps like ones that have proven successful – you want developers who are innovators, not ones that are trying to ride the coattails of another developer.

When it comes to these investments, the best advice that I can give you is to be very careful which of these companies you choose to invest in. Take the time to do your research ahead of time – don't skip this step – or you could be making a bad investment.

Key Takeaways For This Chapter

- Ethereum is a blockchain-based platform that is a lot more powerful than blockchain alone because of the programming language built into it.

- Ethereum allows you to create smart contracts. It also makes it easier for the designers of applications to develop Dapps.

- Ether is the currency used on Ethereum. You can mine for Ether on Ethereum in much the same way you mine for Bitcoins on Blockchain.

- Smart contracts are electronic contracts that execute automatically according to the terms of the contract. They are contracts that are written in a programming language.

- Smart contracts make it possible to do away with middlemen, making it a less expensive way to create a contract. Once the agreement is in place, the execution is automatic.

- One problem with smart contracts is that there is no way to rescind them once in place. There are also the chances that a bug may creep into the coding.

- Decentralized apps, or Dapps, are applications that are delivered directly to the public without the need for a central administrator.

- Ethereum makes a lot simpler to create your own Dapps.

- If you have a good idea for a Dapp, you should create a white paper, create a website and social media pages, start building a following. Once that is done, launch a crowd-sale to raise funds to have it developed.

- Choosing the right developer is essential when it comes to Dapps being successful.

- Initial coin offerings are put in place as another way to raise funds. ICOs can be bought as investments but should be viewed as high risk. It is especially important for you to do your homework with these.

This chapter went through what Ethereum, smart contracts and dapps are. In the next one, we will have a look at the future of the blockchain.

Chapter 8: The Future Of Blockchain

I have talked a little about Bitcoins as a cryptocurrency. I have also spoken a bit about how the increased demand for them has increased their value as well. It is like any other commodity that is traded – more demand means a higher value.

Also like any other commodity, there are limits to the numbers of Bitcoins that are available. Initially, it was said that only 21 million Bitcoins would be issued in total.

At latest count, over 15 million Bitcoins have already been mined. The question that most people are asking is what's next? What happens when there are no new Bitcoins?

There are theories that the whole Bitcoin blockchain will implode - if the miners have no chance of deriving an income from verifying transactions, will they continue to do so?

One solution is the introduction of transaction fees. Another solution would be for more Bitcoins to be issued. Transaction fees make a lot more sense because they are a more sustainable way to continue with Bitcoin.

One thing that Bitcoin has proven is that blockchain is a success. With newer applications like Ethereum growing from strength to strength and developing the blockchain even further, it will be here to stay.

Bitcoin started out as an experiment and has proven very useful in that regard – we can see what worked well and what didn't work at all.

One thing that no one can deny is how innovative the blockchain concept is and how it has turned our standard way of thinking on its head.

That the internet has changed as a result is a certainty and that blockchain is going to continue to change the way we do things online is also definite. Even if you do have reservations, you must admit that this is true.

We have seen some of the world's most significant financial institutions start conducting their own experiments with the technology. That already shows how seriously it is being taken.

Add in that some world governments, like Russia and Brazil, have started using it, and that the EU is planning to regulate cryptocurrencies further and it's clear that cryptocurrencies and blockchain technology are here to stay.

Blockchain has already been hailed as a major disruptor of traditional financial systems – we just don't know how far it will go.

The future for blockchain looks bright as it seems that more people are getting on board with. While it is not yet a household name, that point can't be too far off anymore.

And what is so exciting is that it can be used in so many different applications and ways. Some of the world's best creative minds are working on ways to use this technology to our advantage.

I, for one, can't wait to see what we will be using it for in five or ten years' time.

Here are some of the things that I predict we can expect.

The Internet Of Things

This is one concept that I am really excited about and that's why I'm going into more detail about what it could be like. We have already seen some examples of this in action already. You can get a smart kettle that you can set to boil using your phone when you are five minutes out.

But the internet of things is so much bigger than this. Just look at how useful a Smart TV is, for example. You don't need a set-top box to stream Netflix or YouTube anymore, you and your whole family can watch your favorite shows with the click of a few buttons on your TV.

Now, imagine that kind of functionality in everything from your car, your fridge, your washer, and dryer, to your stereo system will have its own IP address. You could stream music directly to your stereo system.

You could send your friend videos or music for them to listen to on their TV or stereo instantly. Your TV will truly become a full entertainment center.

Your fridge could even end up smarter than you. It could, for example, scan every soda can in the refrigerator and warn you that you are running low. You could even program it to order groceries for you automatically.

And you would have your own self-driving smart car. So, the fridge could place the order, and the car could go and collect it. (Okay, so, logistically that may be going a little far, but you can see how it might work.)

Let's look at something a little more practical – your self-driven car could talk to that of your spouse to determine who is in a better position to fetch the kids from school that day.

Car accidents and unruly behavior on the road should be reduced. One thing that I think might be quite amusing is to see how road rage changes. If your car is driving and you want to get somewhere in a hurry, I would imagine that that would be an interesting looking conversation.

I can see myself having an argument with my car about the best direction to take or how long the drive is taking.

So, how far off might this be? We could be talking about this kind of thing in less than ten years.

As mentioned before, the major problem with instituting this type of thing was that each company would have to have a centralized server to support these new appliances.

Cost-wise, there is not enough benefit to the company for that to happen. Regarding computing power alone, the costs would be staggering. And the system would have to be very secure.

It's not going to matter too much if someone hacks your refrigerator or kettle, but what happens with things that would be more valuable to thieves, like your car?

The other issue with having centralized servers would be if the servers went down. Your car and other appliances just would not work.

Can you imagine how chaotic it would be in rush hour traffic if the servers suddenly went down and your car could no longer drive itself? Can you imagine how many accidents would occur as a result?

Personally, if I were manufacturing smart cars, I would not want that kind of responsibility.

But blockchain makes this a lot easier. With apps being developed that enable people to rent out the extra space on their hard drives, is it inconceivable that they would be willing to join a blockchain network and earn money in exchange for using their computing power?

Blockchain users are already able to be rewarded for helping with verifications by mining Bitcoins. What if earning some money was guaranteed and a lot simpler than mining? I know that a lot more people would be interested if it was.

The blockchain is more secure than a centralized server would be, and changes submitted to the system would have to undergo a verification process anyway.

Also, if you have so much more nodes within the system, the chances that the system is going to experience downtime decreases.

It Will Be Easier To Check The Origin Of Goods

More people now take an interest in how the goods they purchase are being produced/ grown. They want to know that the goods that they are buying are produced regarding Fair Trade agreements and in an environmentally responsible way.

Now, you only have the suppliers word that this is the case. They will show pictures of the goods being produced or grown, but how do you know that this is an accurate reflection?

We also know that goods that are marketed as "fresh" might not be anywhere close to as fresh as we think they are because cold storage and chemicals can be used to extend the shelf-life.

Remember when we were saying that blockchain was transforming the supply chain industry? This is something that I believe is going to become even more important in future, especially for the consumers.

With this kind of system in place within the blockchain, clients can see exactly where their goods are coming from, how long they took to get to the store, etc.

The blockchain can make it easy for consumers to check these issues and become more informed. Businesses will benefit by fostering better client relationships and increasing the trust in their brand.

Many people feel that companies have become untrustworthy as regards the sourcing of goods, etc. For those people, blockchain offers a viable solution.

Online Security

Hacking of personal information is something that hackers are good at. They can make a lot of money with that information and so they will always be trying to get it.

If they can, they will use that information to get your money as well. Anti-hacking measures are getting more advanced, but so are hackers.

Think of it this way. You decide to store all your valuables in a bank vault. They have great security and, to be honest, much better security than you have at home. They have guards, alarms, time-delay locks, passcodes, and keys.

Despite all this, if a bank robber is organized enough and has the right tools, they can get into that vault. What's more tempting for them to rob? Your home, or the bank vault?

Robbing the bank is harder but a lot more rewarding than burglarizing one person's home.

Keeping all your client's information in one spot makes a very tempting and profitable target for hackers.

As children, we were told, "You must not keep all your eggs in one basket." It's amazing how we veered away from that concept when it comes to our online safety, isn't it?

Blockchain can and will get us back on track, I believe. You can use the same high encryptions to protect the information within the blockchain. The verification process makes it much harder for hackers to randomly introduce fraudulent transactions.

And, most importantly, with the information spread to so many different nodes, hackers would have to realistically hack all the nodes at the same time if they wanted to rewrite a blockchain string from scratch or if they wanted to change it.

It just is nowhere near as easy for the hacker to get at the information or change anything when it is in a blockchain.

The blockchain is simple and effective.

Intelligent Application Of The Technology

One area that I see changing in future is the information that is out there about blockchain. I think that part of the reason that we haven't seen it become a much more mainstream idea up to now is that people don't know about it and don't understand how it works.

That's changing, though. Twitter and Square CEO, Jack Dorsey, described blockchain as being the "next big unlock"[3] in an interview in August of 2017. He went on to say that the potential for blockchain was huge.

He also cautioned against trying to use blockchain in everything and anything. His advice was for us to start asking what it is that people need.

He is correct. It is not something that should be applied to everything and, if you try to do that, the system could fall short. We have also to consider what the effect would be of adding hundreds of thousands or even millions of new users.

There has been an increase in interest in the technology, and more specifically Bitcoin, recently. Dorsey mentioned that he had a few people that he knew, people not at all related to the tech industry, ask him about Bitcoins and whether they should invest.

If you keep a pulse on social media, it is something that seems to have been getting a lot more play lately. It makes sense that if people are becoming more interested in Bitcoin, they'll want to know about blockchain as well.

---

[3] https://www.theverge.com/2017/8/11/16126610/square-twitter-founder-jack-dorsey-blockchain-bitcoin-banks

More Information

I think we will see a lot more information about the blockchain and how it works coming in future. I believe that this information will also be scaled down so that the average person is much more easily able to understand the concept.

I have a techie background, and I have been interested in this topic for a while. I must admit, though, that some of the books I have read on the subject are advanced for a beginner and require some specialized knowledge to read.

I think that's going to start changing now. I have tried, with this book, to give you something that is easy to understand because I realize that not everyone reading this book will have a background in tech.

I think others are going to be doing the same.

Will The Sharing Economy Be Rebooted With Blockchain?

Airbnb and Uber are two examples of how the sharing economy works. They were hailed a new way of doing things, but they haven't really lived up to that promise.

Issues with the costs of running the online platform required for these kinds of companies can be a barrier to entry for a small startup. The use of blockchain could help to alleviate these costs.

The introduction of smart contracts could also make the overall process less expensive and easier to manage. The combination of the internet of things + blockchain + the sharing economy I think will be the most exciting thing to watch.

Let's say that I rent out my home, for example. I must give out my key to the person renting the home. This can be a pain in itself – it means that I must be there to let them in, no matter what time they arrive and I also must be there when they leave. It also means that they could make a copy of the key and use it to access the property after they have left.

If on the other hand, I have an electronic lock that I can program, there would be no need for me to be there when they arrive or when they leave. I could program the lock so that they are admitted, and once they leave, it locks behind them.

It's trivial things like this, plus the reduced operating costs and increased efficiency of blockchain systems that could reboot the sharing economy industry in future.

Shared investment opportunities could be a new incarnation of the sharing economy. MyBit[4] is an example of a platform that allows investors to invest in stakes of what they title "revenue generating machines."

It's crowdfunding, combined with smart assets, which enables smaller investors to buy a stake in a machine. The machine will be built, and the investor will receive a portion

---

[4] https://mybit.io/

of the revenue realized by that machine. This will be managed in a blockchain system.

The aim is to eventually branch out into things such as self-driving cars, drones, etc. but for now the company is focusing on clean energy in general, and solar panels in particular.

The company's first project is to help fund the building of microgrids that will be able to operate entirely separately of the central power grids. The idea is that the microgrids will also be able to produce excess electricity that can be sold to the central grids or on the open market.

Founded under similar principles is Slock.it. The aim here is to make it possible for people to share, rent or sell any smart object that is connected to the network. Also underwritten by Ethereum Blockchain technology, the aim is to shake up the sharing economy.

Tracking Of Guns

Keeping track of guns, especially considering recent events in the United States, makes sense. Logging guns into a blockchain based system would make it a lot easier to create a registry where information about all gun sales could be accessed by law enforcers or the owners of the weapons.

At the moment, a company called BlockSafe is using this technology to help the owners of guns keep track of whether lost guns have been fired.

Deceased Estates

A will is a kind of contract that is well-suited to the use of smart contracts. I think we will see a lot more cases where wills are drawn up as smart contracts.

Doing this would make some aspects of the handling of the will easier regarding factual aspects. Like, for example, someone claims that her dear old Aunt Violet left her all her jewelry. The claim could be dismissed out of hand if no provision is left in the will.

Blockchain Technologies Corp is working on a system that would end up being self-executing when it came to deceased estates in the United States. The blockchain will first verify the death against the "Death Master File administered by the government before beginning to execute the will.

This would cut the need to prove that the person has died. The person will set up the system to distribute the assets to those named automatically. There will be no need to have an executor manage the estate, and this should reduce the infighting amongst heirs over the validity of the stipulations in the will.

Of course, there is some work that needs to be done. Can the system automatically calculate and pay over the death duties and debts claimed against the estate? How would it deal with cases where assets would have to be sold? Would the system be able to place all the notifications as required by law?

Some of the processes can indeed be automated. How much of it can remain to be seen?

Retail

Most of us shop with trusted online retailers because we know that our credit card details are safe with them. In other instances, we use a payment system like Paypal to pay.

But what if we do not have the option to pay by Paypal and we are unwilling to give out our credit card details?

OpenBazaar is one of the startups that is dealing with that issue. It is a platform that allows sellers to pay in whatever cryptocurrency they like. The merchants are not restricted regarding what they can sell and are not charged transaction fees. The merchants are paid in Bitcoin.

Charitable Donations More Transparent

We all love donating money to charity but how do you know that the money you are giving makes it to where it was supposed to go?

With a blockchain-based system, you would be able to track the money that you have given and see how much actually was used for the intended purpose and whether there was any wastage.

The BitGive Foundation is an example of how this could work. It allows donors more insight into how much money has been received and how it is used. This can help the charity to build credibility and trust with their donors.

The Prosecution Of Crimes

When it comes to the prosecution of crimes, it is essential to maintain a proper chain of evidence. As the blockchain is not easy to alter, it makes a pretty good way to record evidence and to ensure the proper handling of the evidence.

The blockchain can also be used to flag suspicious transactions across cryptocurrencies.

Human Resources

If you can automate as much of the background checking process as possible when hiring someone, you can save a lot of time and prevent human error from creeping in.

If all criminal records and employment records are placed in a specific blockchain, running these checks could be a lot easier and faster. You would not need to call anyone to confirm employment dates and the system could be set to scan for a criminal history.

Getting Paid For Work

It's a bit of a foreign concept for most of us, but you do not have to receive your salary in a bank account or cash. You could opt for it to be paid in cryptocurrencies instead.

Now, most of us have bills to pay, so we need that money in the account but what if you are working a second job? Or working just so that you can save money for a car, or something like that?

You could be paid in a cryptocurrency and your choice would either be to spend the money or to leave it where it is.

You could use the salary to speculate a little – you could leave it there in the hopes that the cryptocurrency value would rise. Imagine, Bitcoins were worth next to nothing when they first came out; now one Bitcoin is worth thousands.

Of course, if you do go this route, things could also go the other way – the currency could be devalued as well.

Key Takeaways For This Chapter

- The future of blockchain looks bright.

- There are thoughts that it might reinvigorate the sharing economy.

- It can be turned to several purposes from the automatic processing of will through to the prosecution of crimes.

- One of the most exciting probabilities is that it will make the Internet of Things possible to achieve.

Conclusion

Thanks again for taking the time to purchase this book!

You should now have a good understanding of blockchain, and be able to understand how fascinating the implications of this technology are.

I hope I have inspired you to learn more about Blockchain and Ethereum and to keep an eye on new developments in the media. Who knows, maybe your next contract will be set up and executed on Ethereum!

More than anything else, I hope I have inspired you to take a closer look at the technologies that are changing the way we do things and seeing whether you have some ideas on how to make them even better.

If you enjoyed this book, please take the time to leave me a review on Amazon. I appreciate your honest feedback, and it helps me to continue producing high-quality books.

About The Author

31-year-old Ikuya Takashima is a Software Developer, entrepreneur, investor and author.

Ikuya first entered the world of Cryptocurrency in 2014 when he finally decided to invest in Bitcoin after several years of following the online currency. Ikuya is now a Cryptocurrency expert & enthusiast with an impressive Cryptocurrency portfolio and investments in several Bitcoin & Ethereum startups.

Ikuya's latest venture is to share his knowledge and passion on the world of Cryptocurrencies with the goal of making seemingly complex and intimidating topics simple and easy-to-read.

In Ikuya's spare time he likes to read, travel and spend time with family and friends

Also by Ikuya Takashima

Cryptocurrency: How I Paid my 6 Figure Divorce Settlement by Cryptocurrency Investing, Cryptocurrency Trading
(available on Amazon)

Ethereum: The Ultimate Guide to the World of Ethereum, Ethereum Mining, Ethereum Investing, Smart Contracts, Dapps and DAOs, Ether, Blockchain Technology
(available on Amazon)

Bitcoin: The Ultimate Guide to the World of Bitcoin, Bitcoin Mining, Bitcoin Investing, Blockchain Technology, Cryptocurrency
(available on Amazon)

Printed in Great Britain
by Amazon